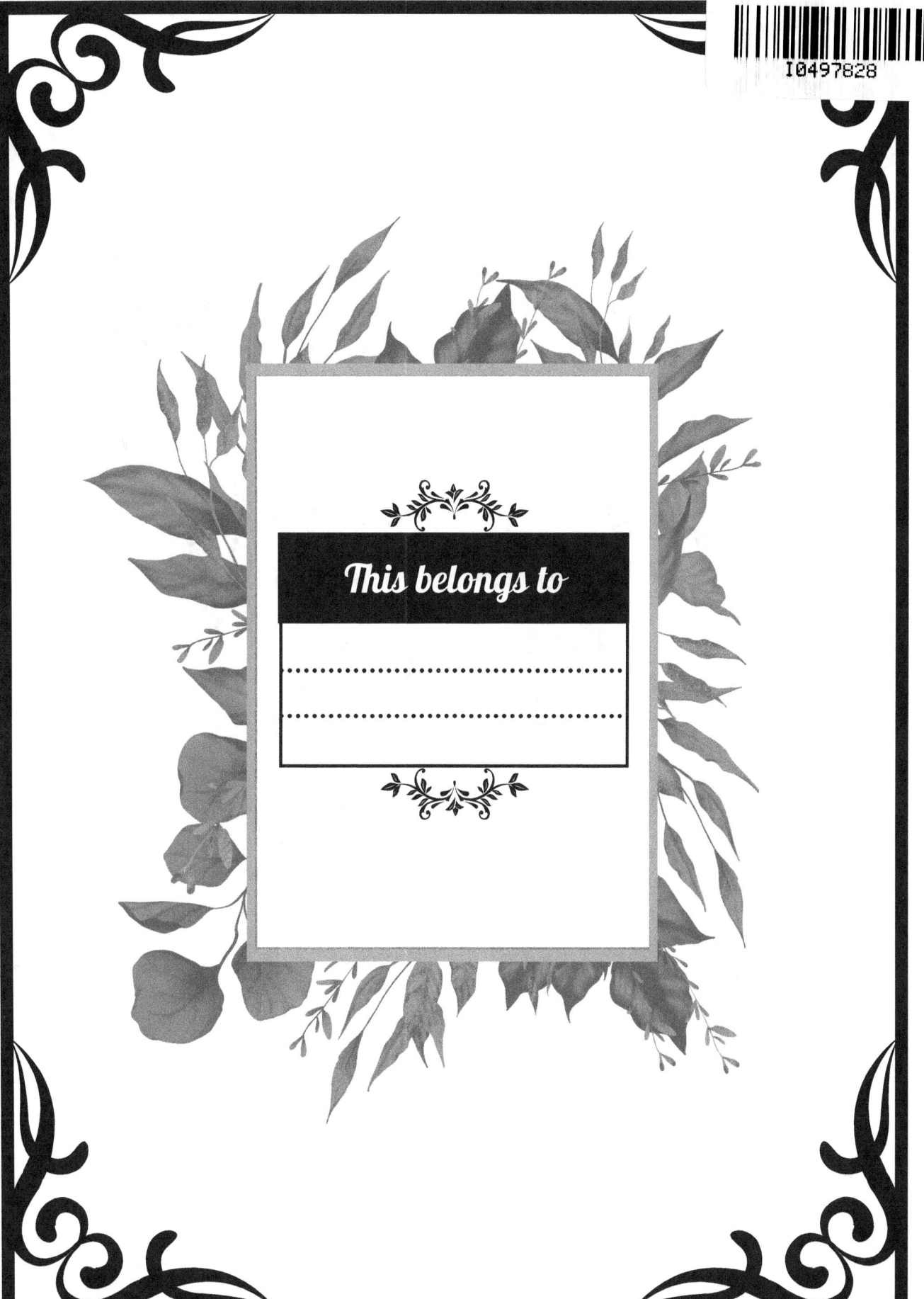

This belongs to

....

....

Lizard

Coloring Book

For Kids

Copyright© 2022
All Rights Reserved By "Jhonson Publication"

Test your Color

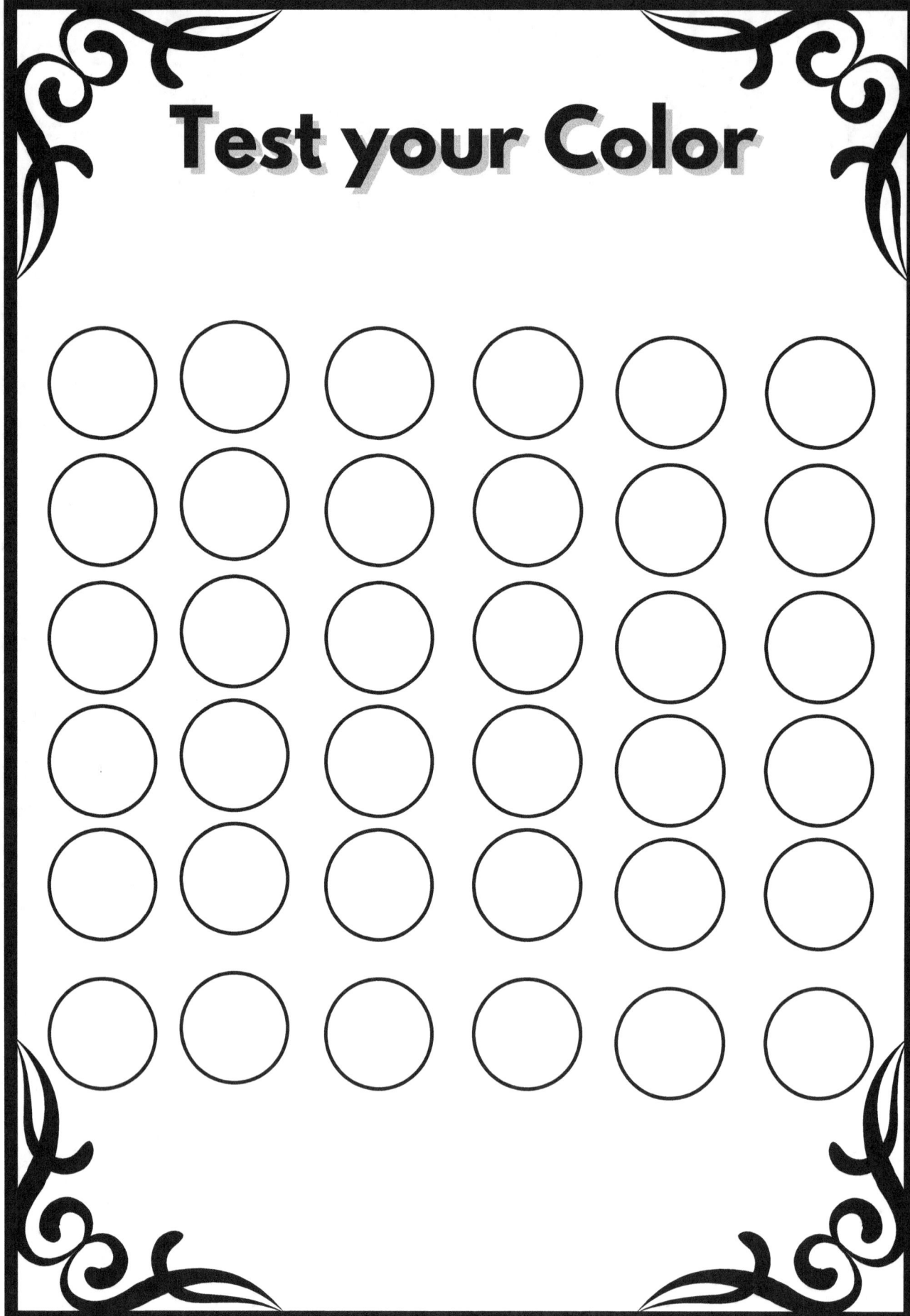

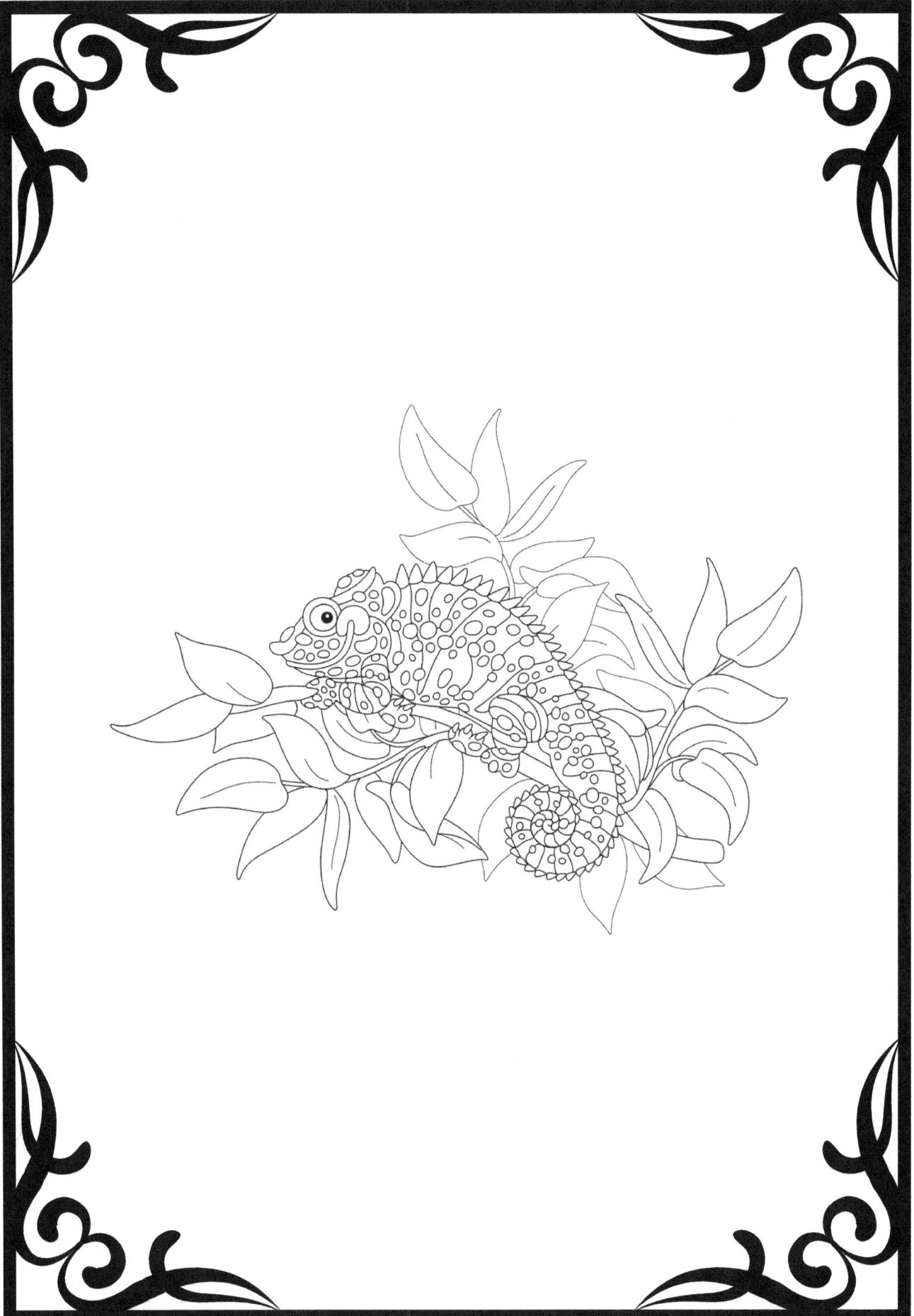

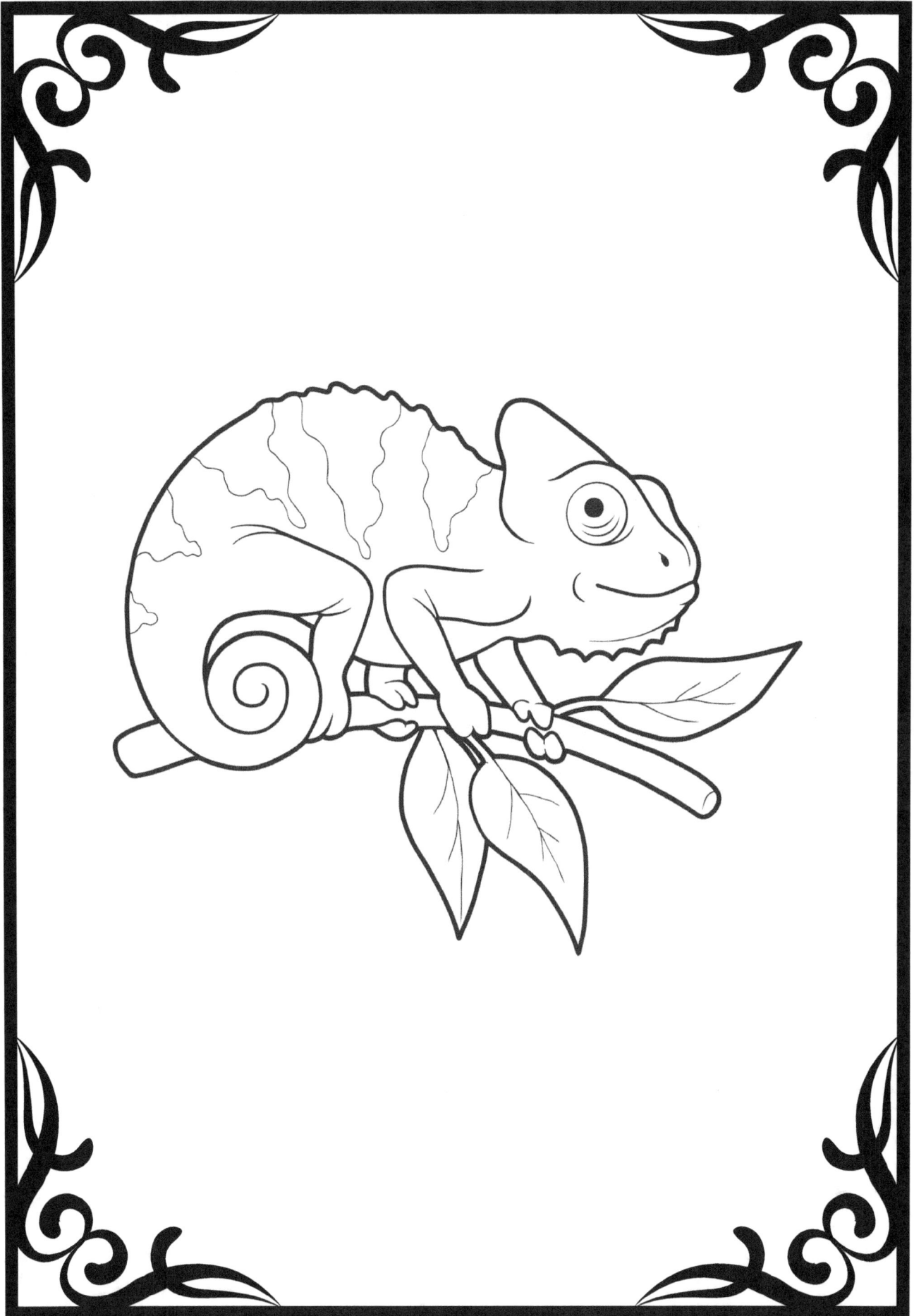

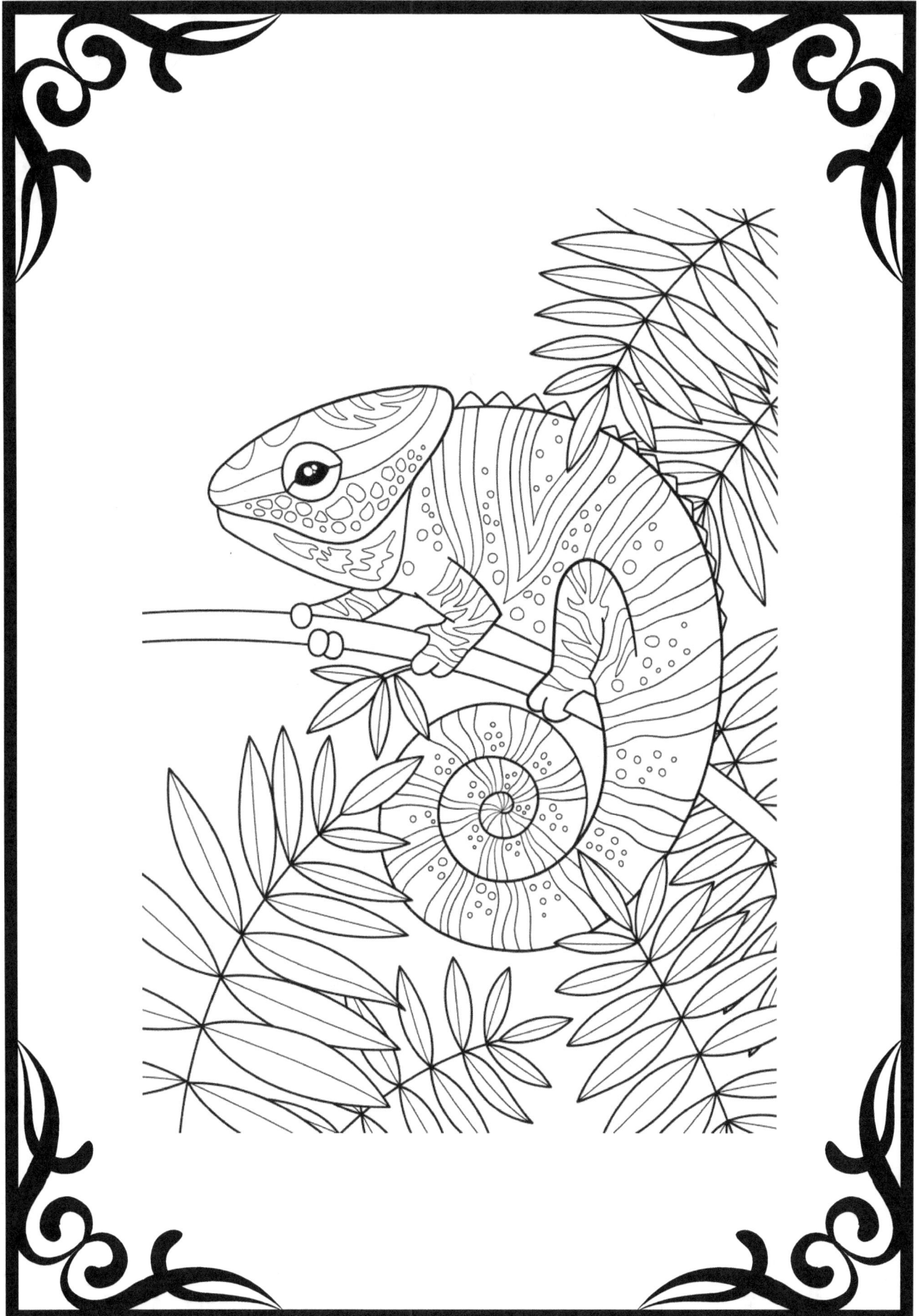

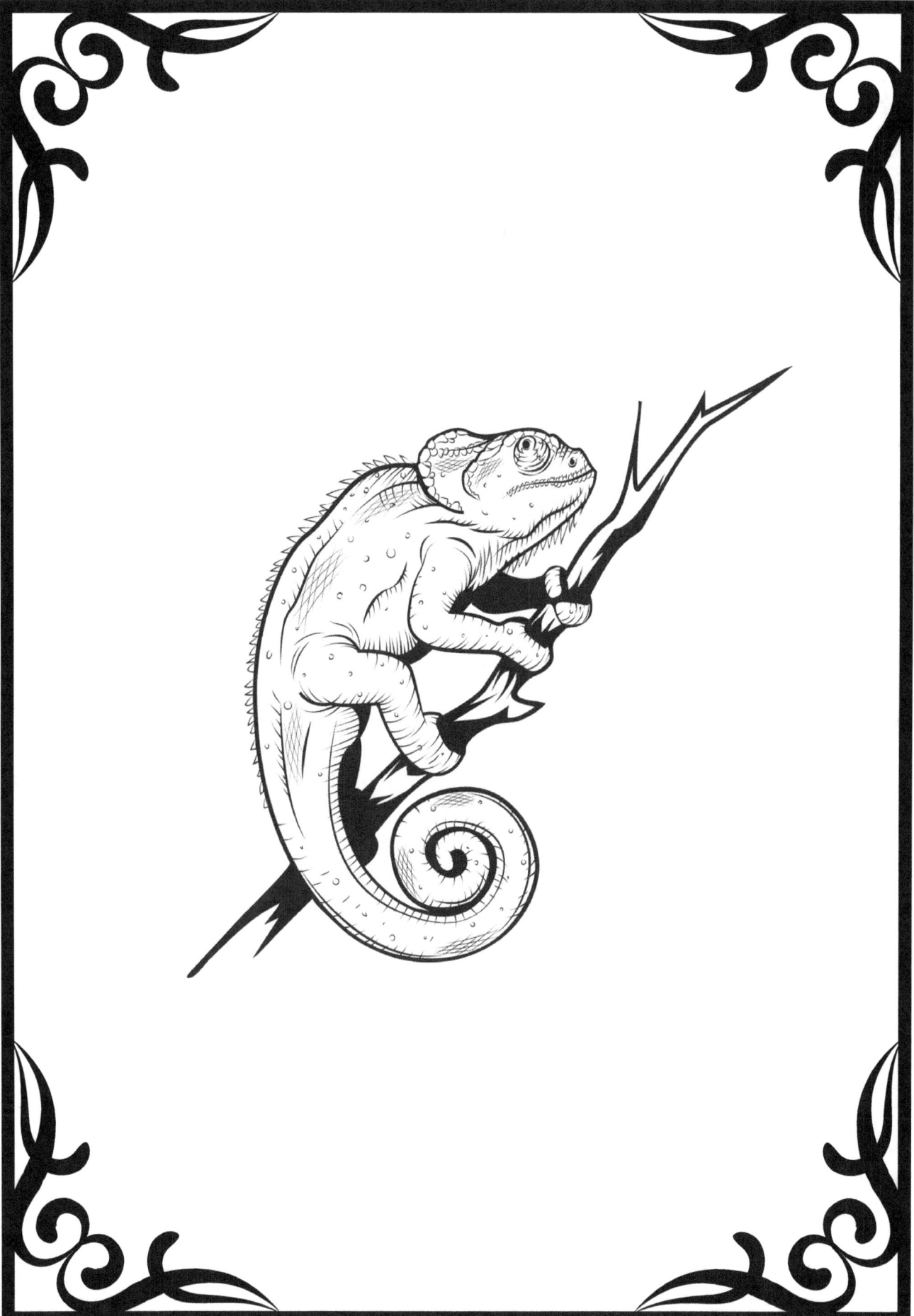

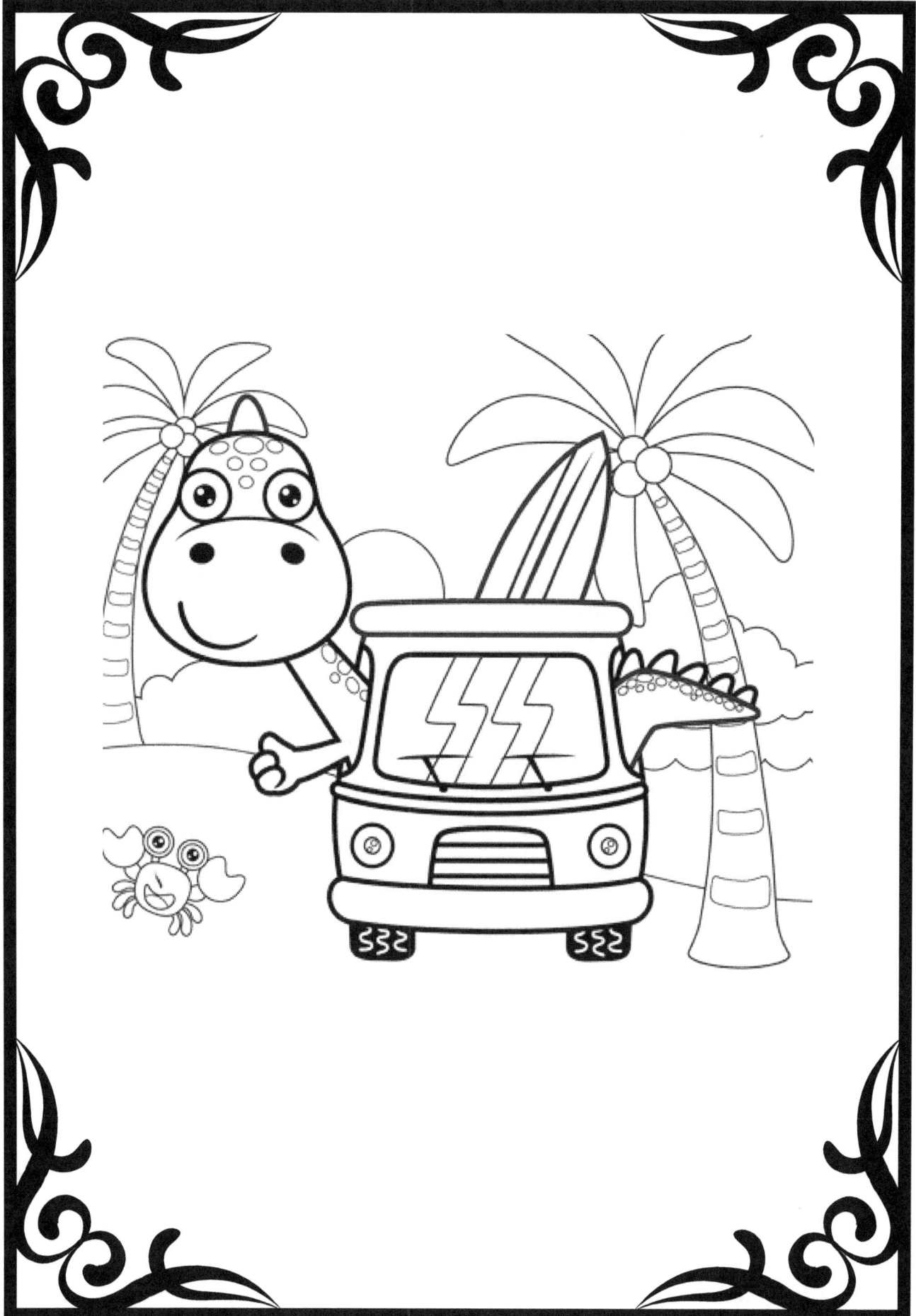

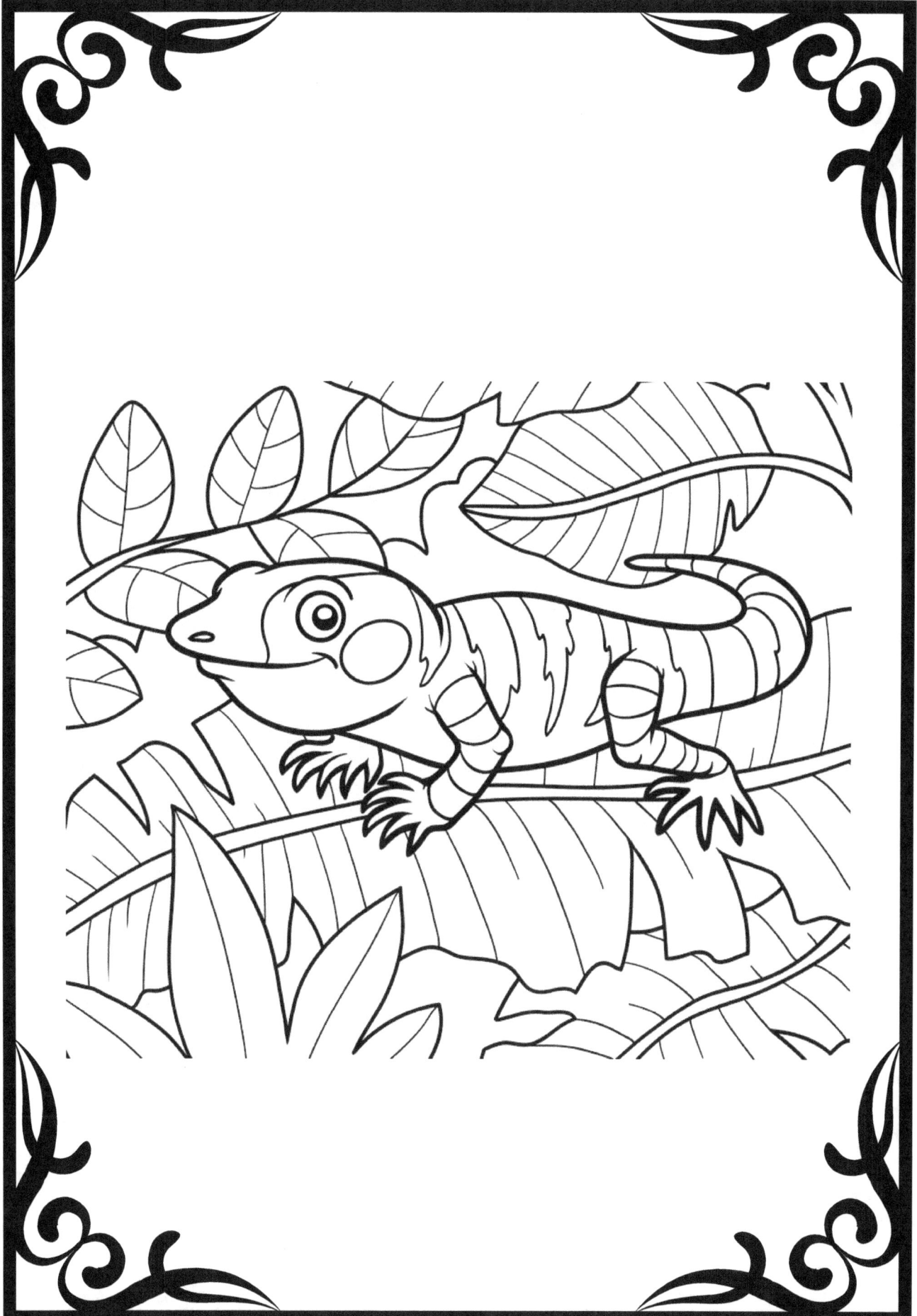

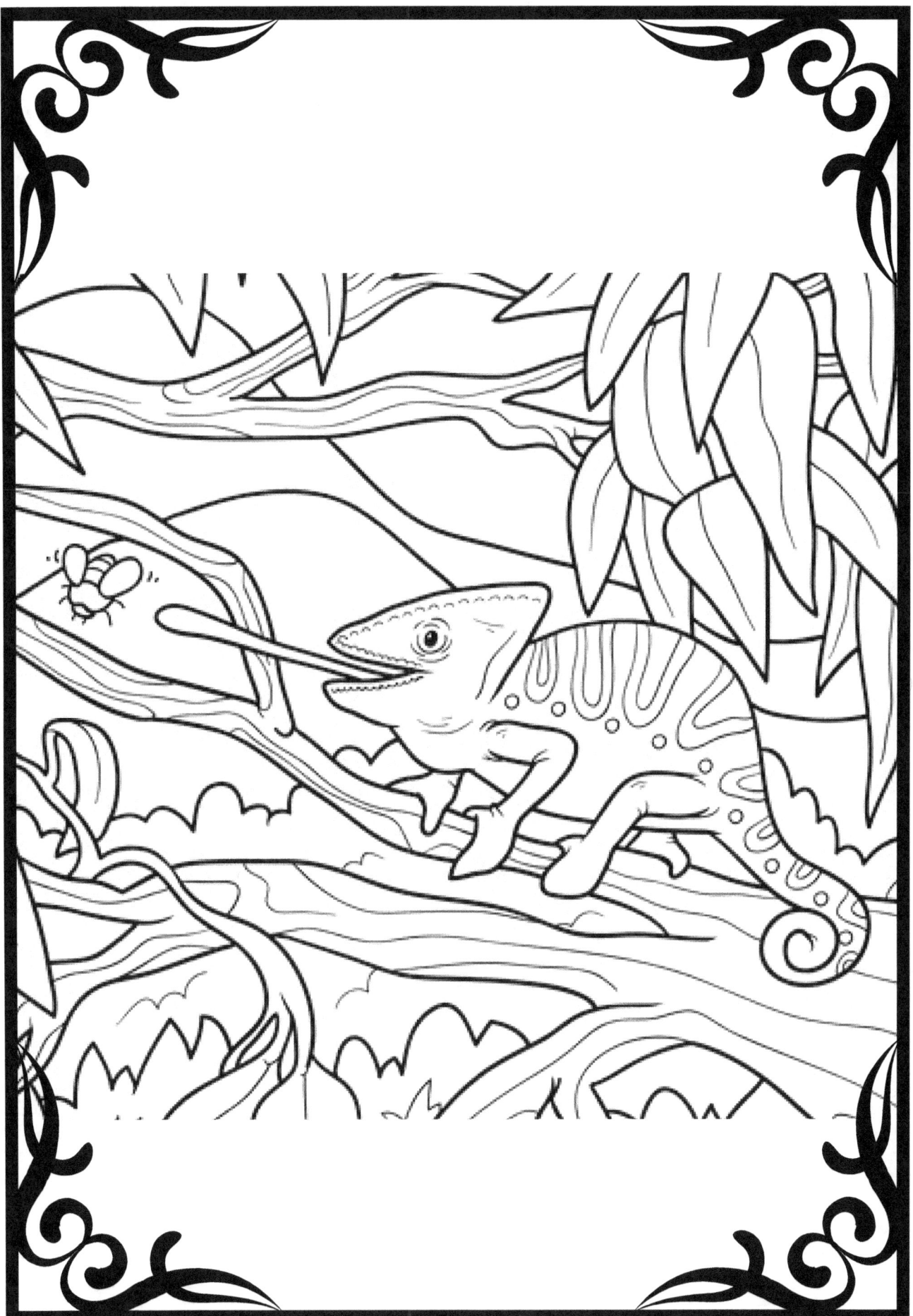

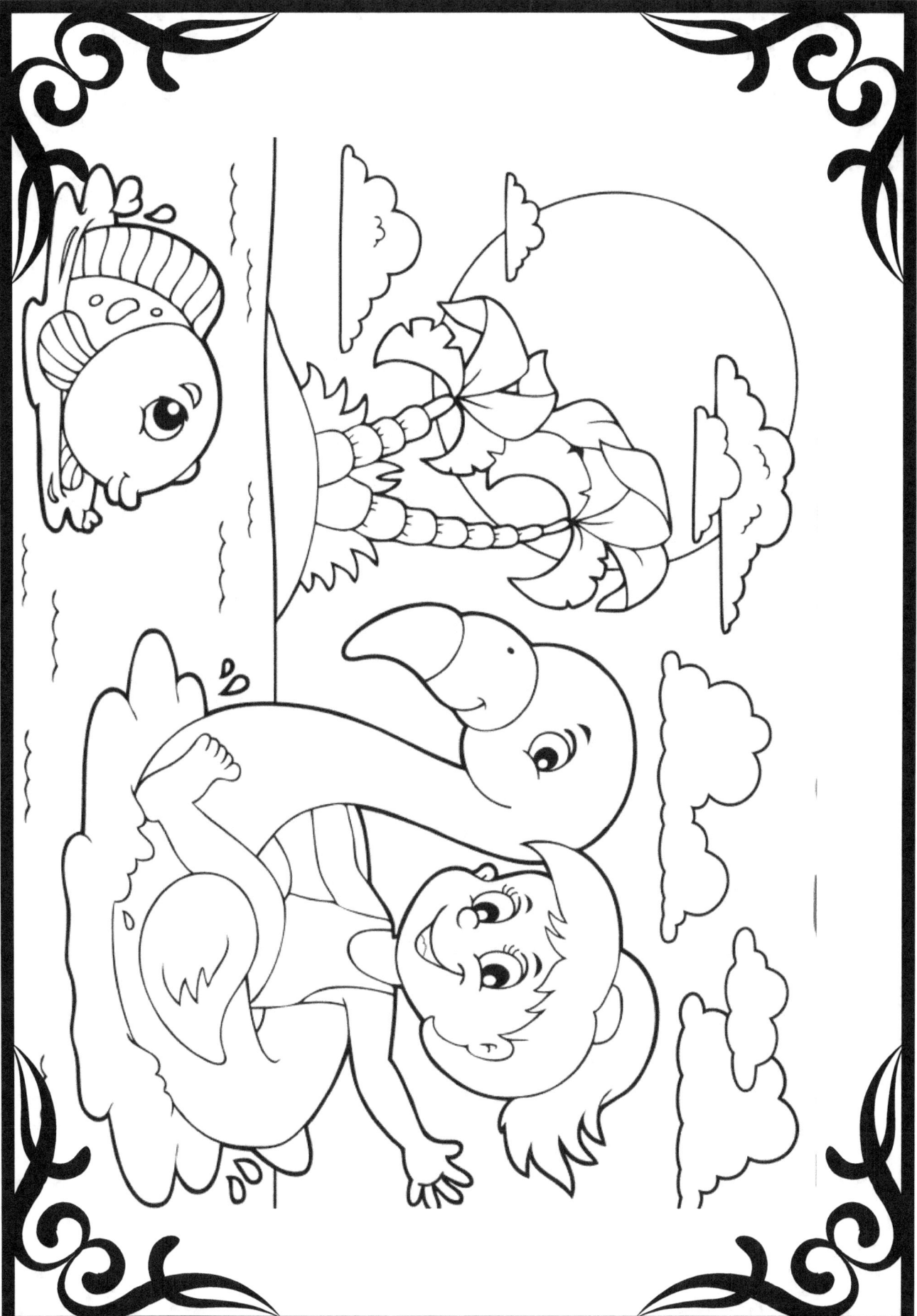

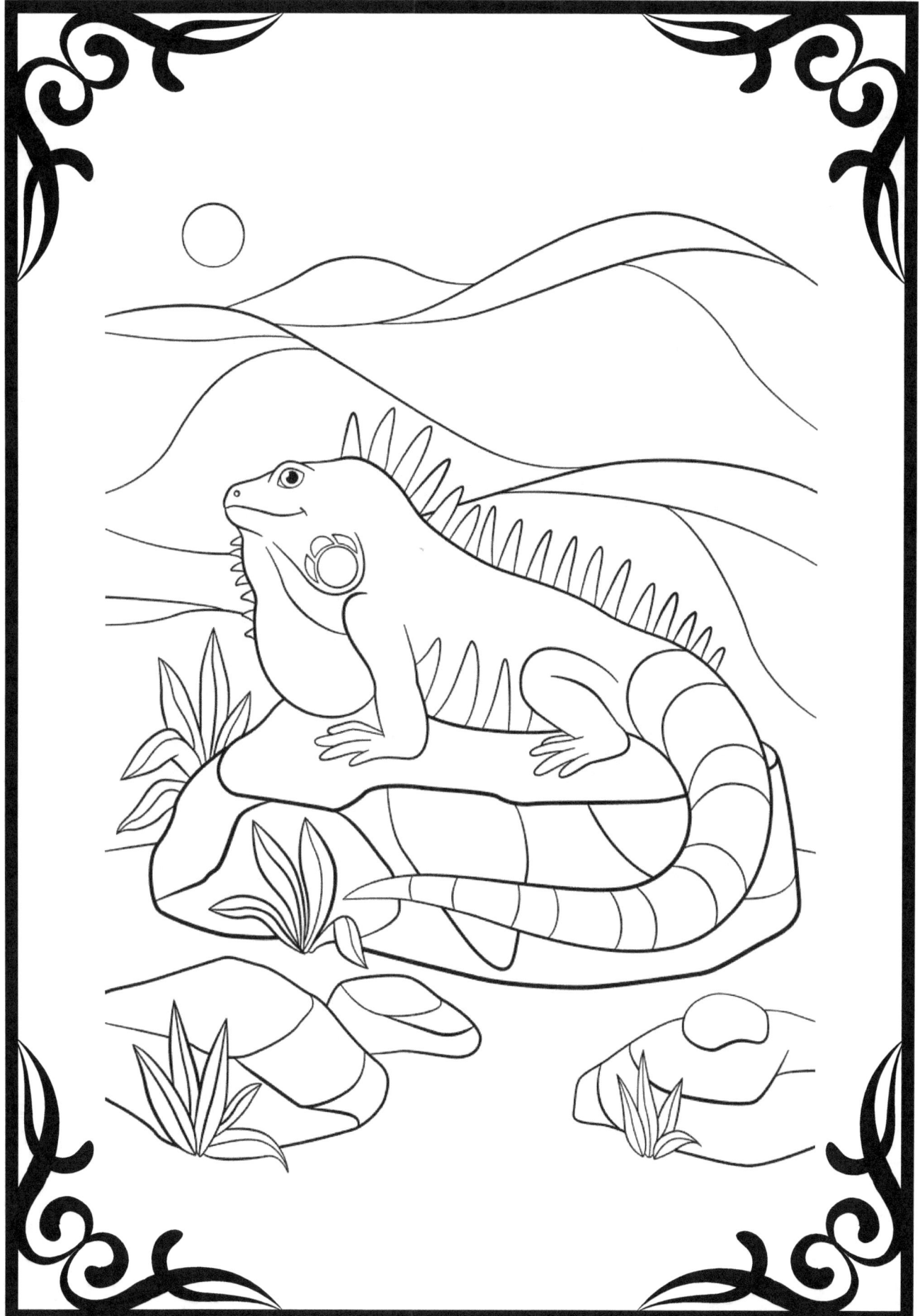

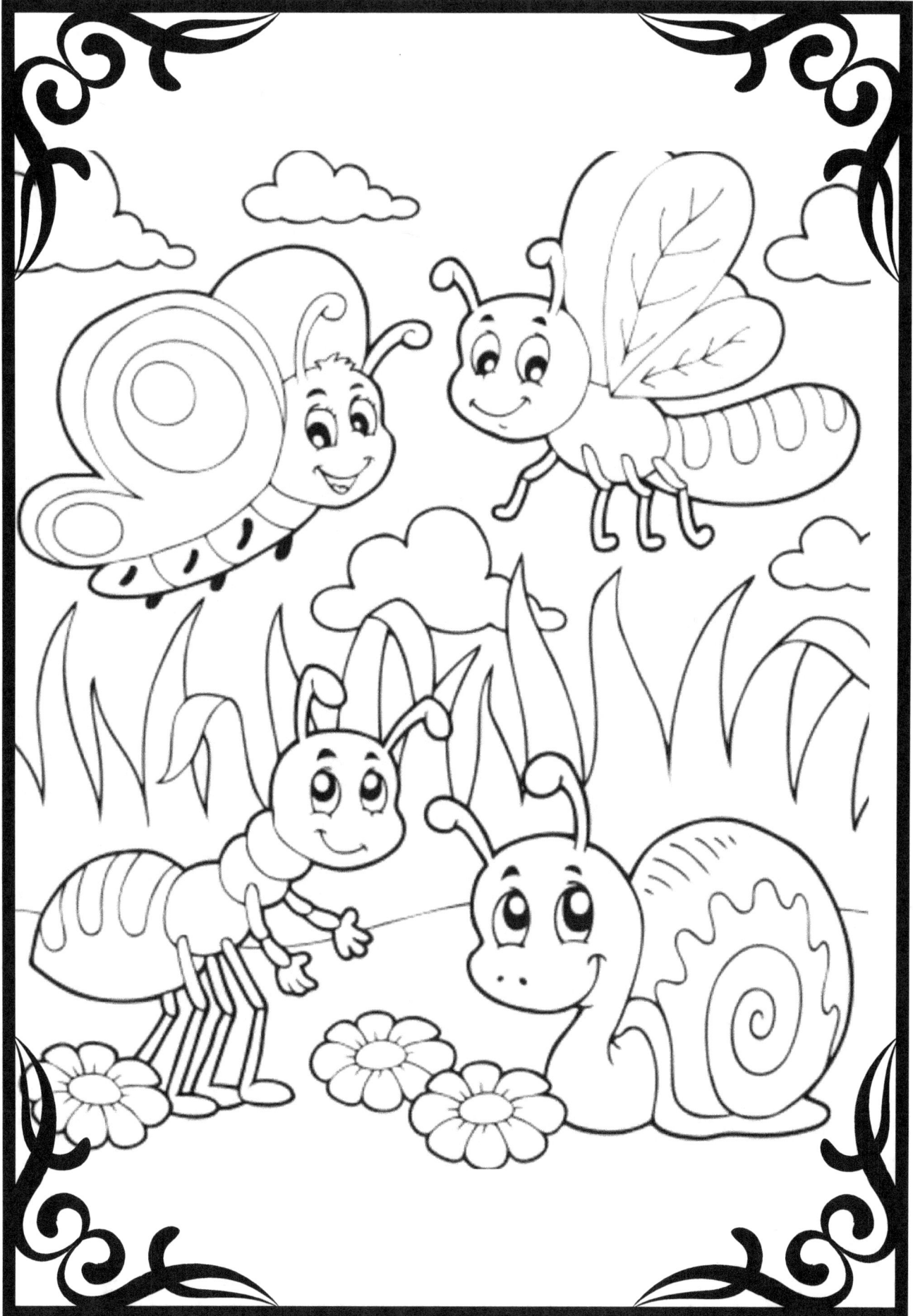

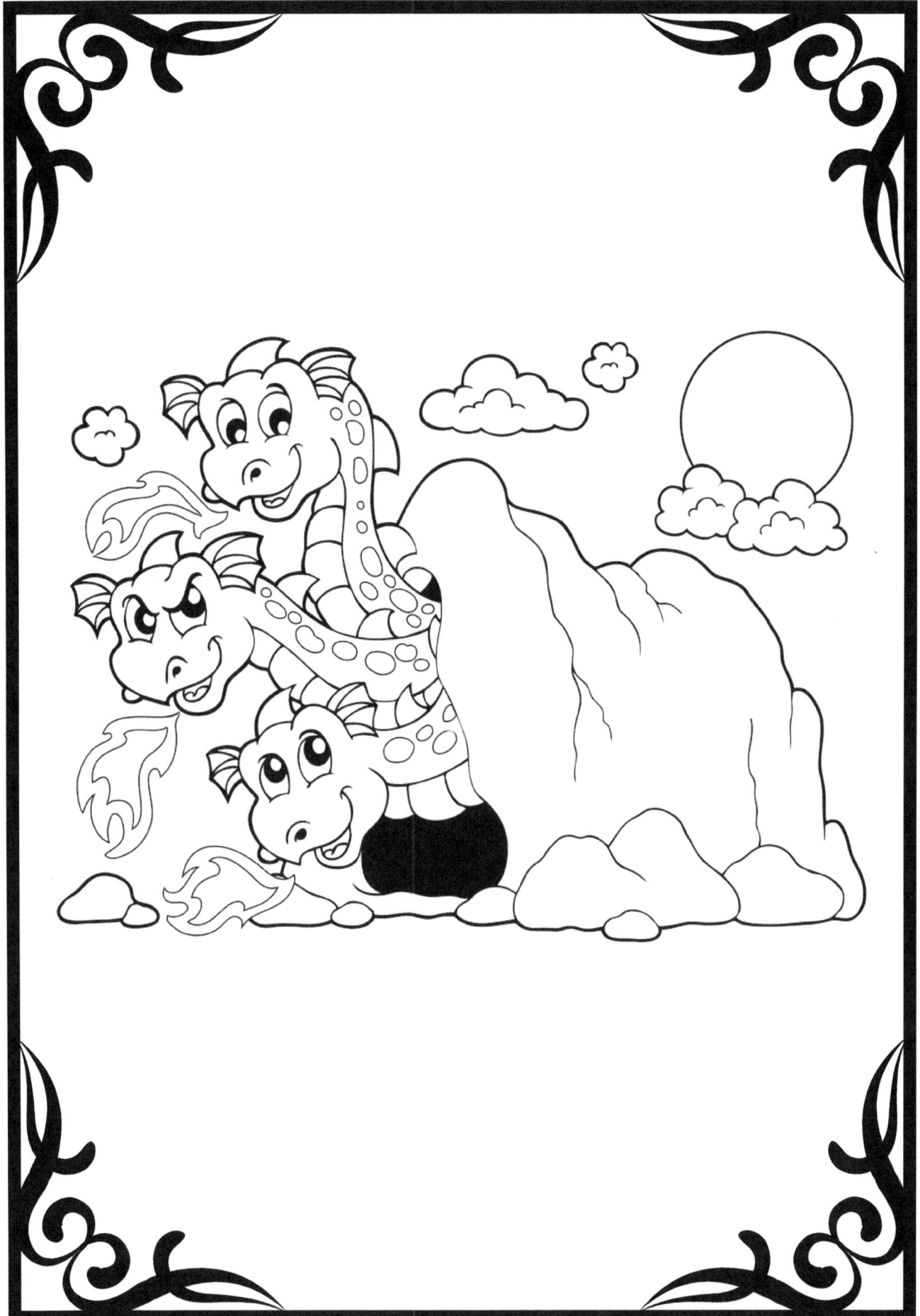

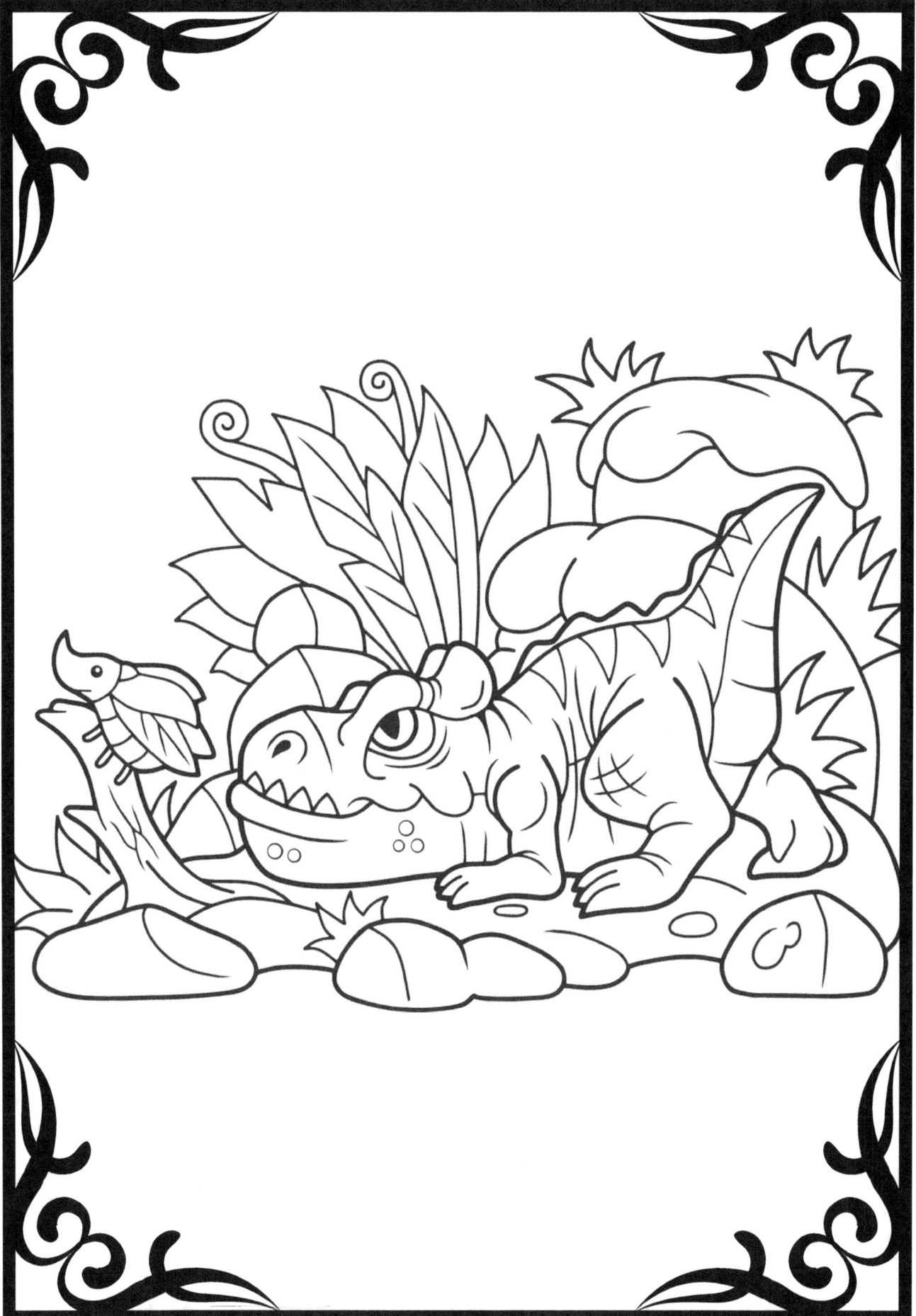

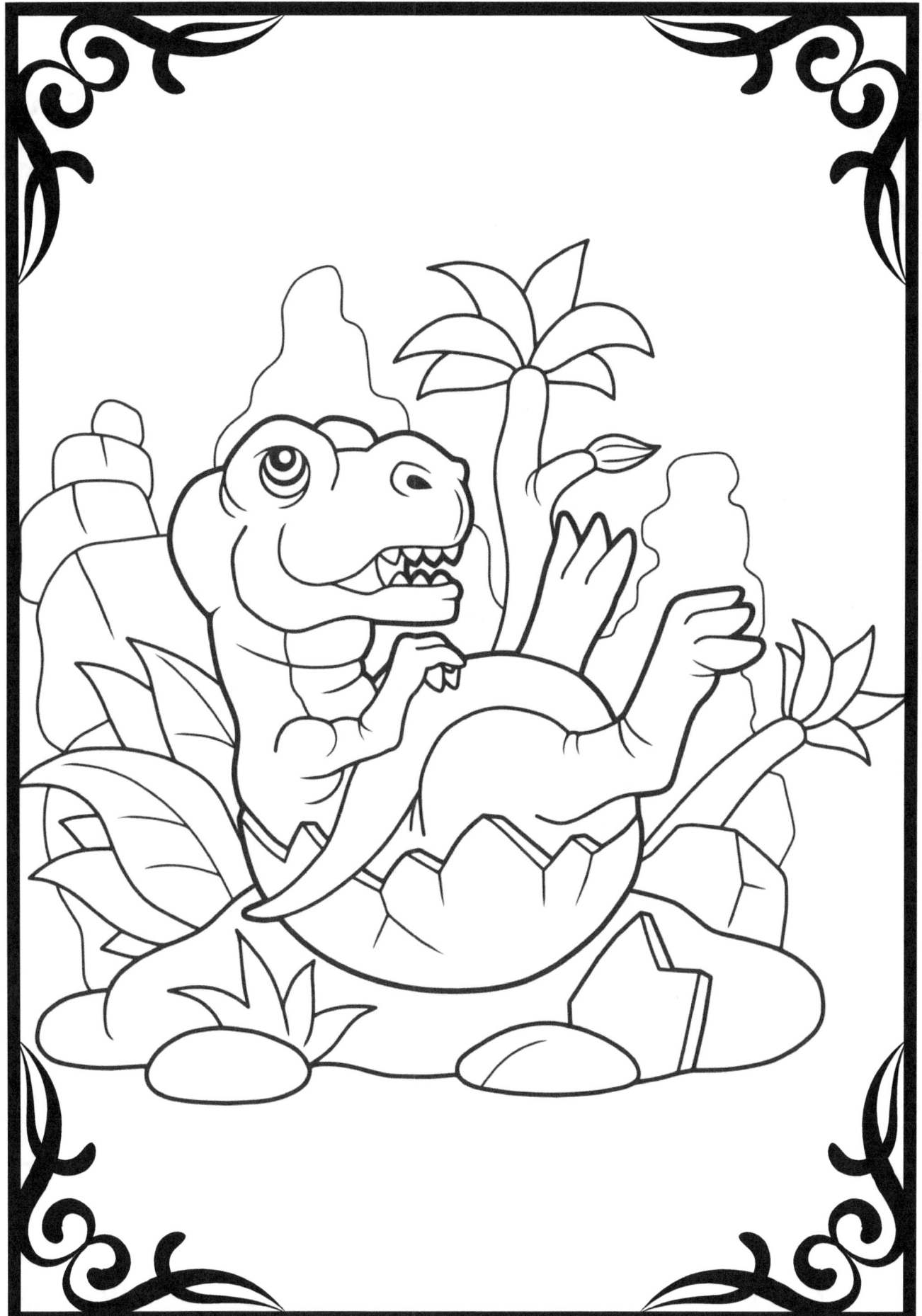

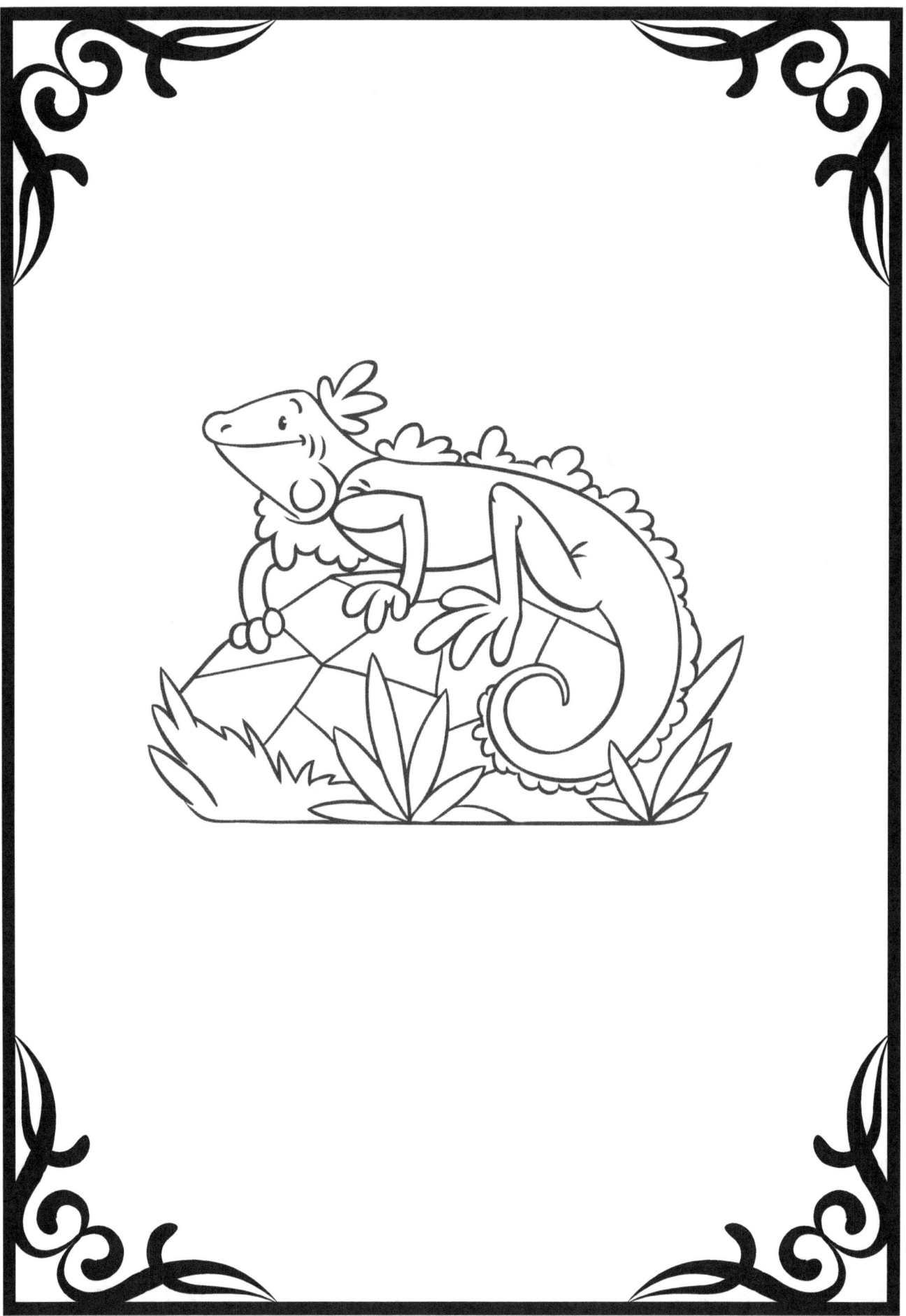

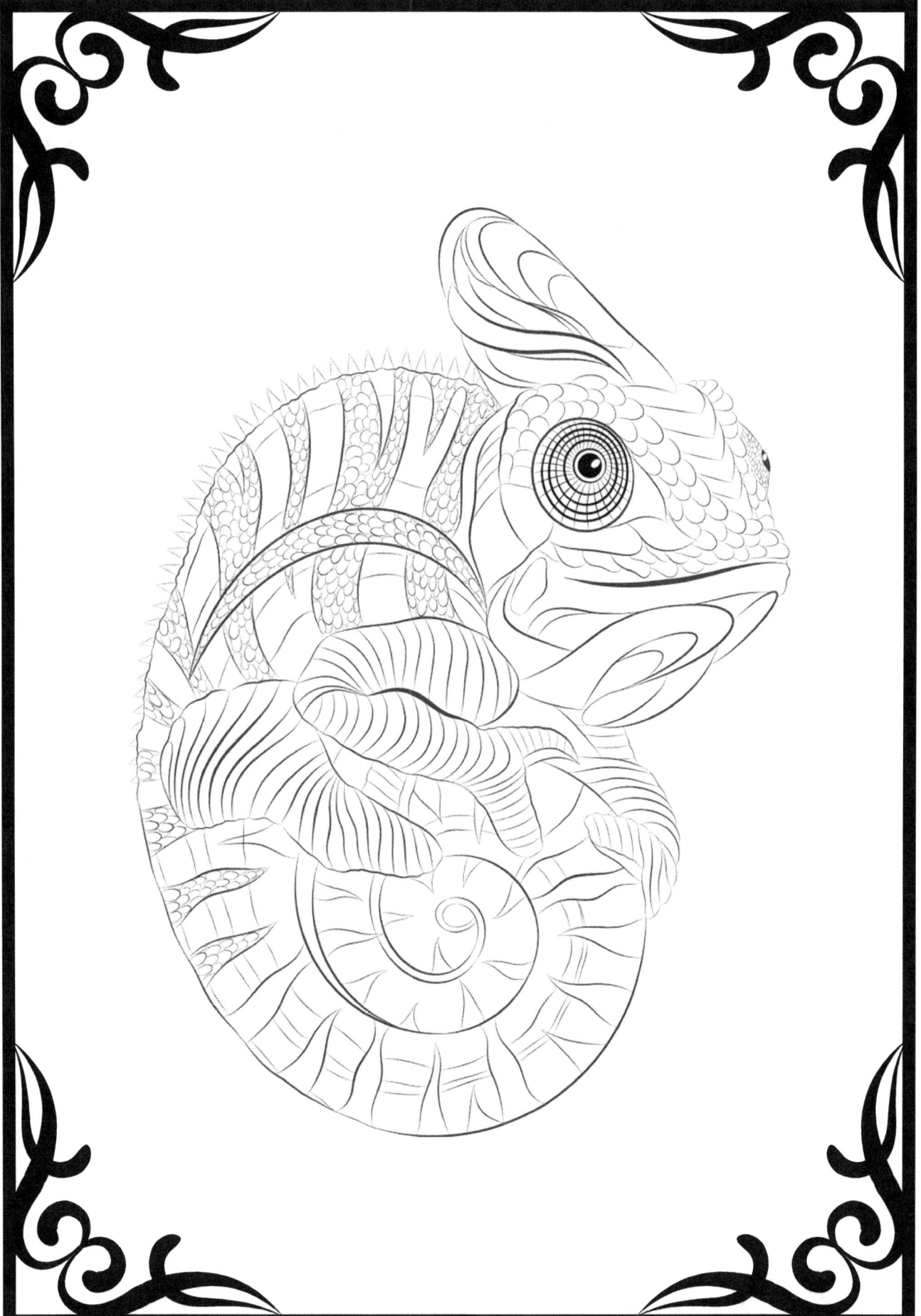

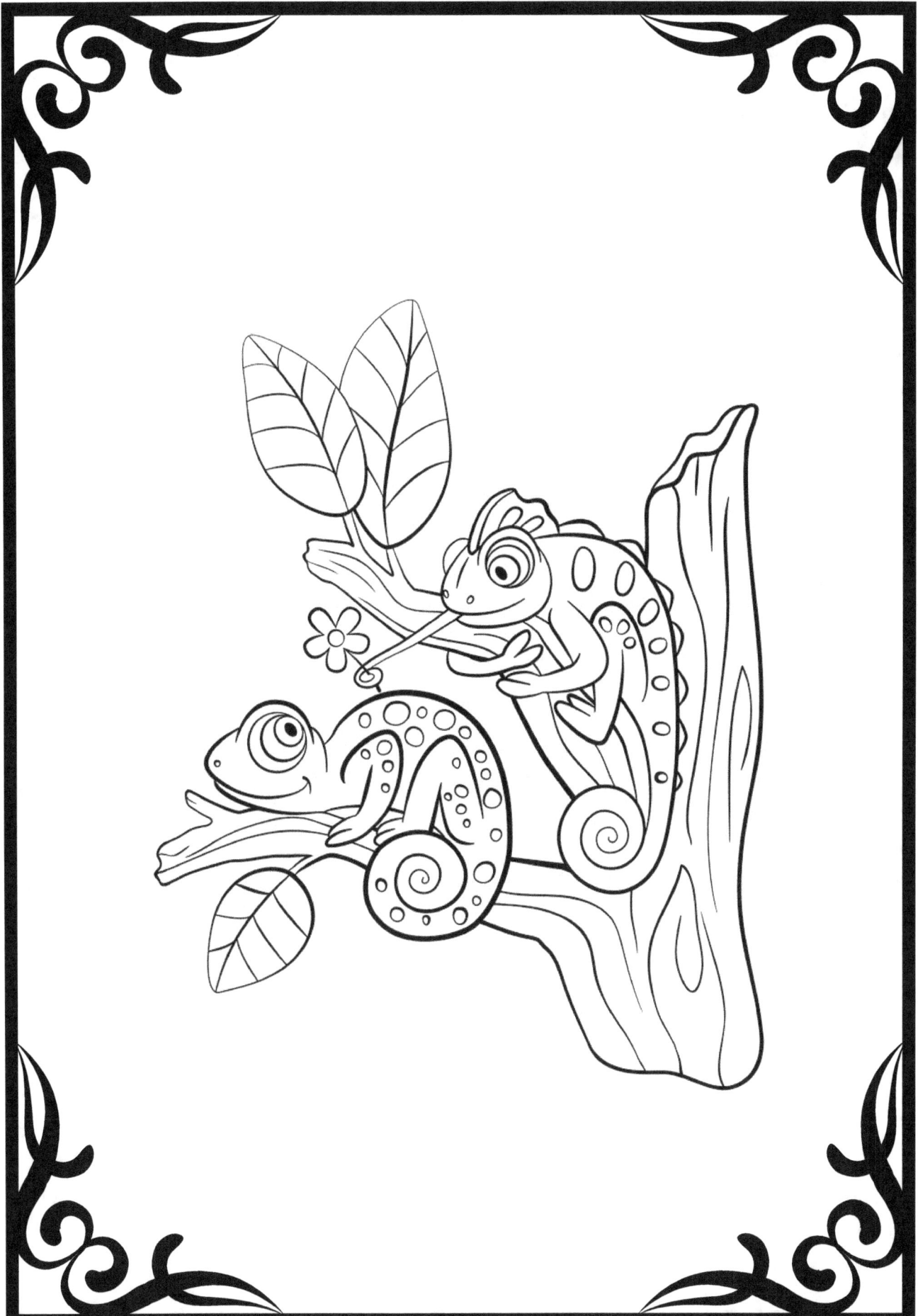

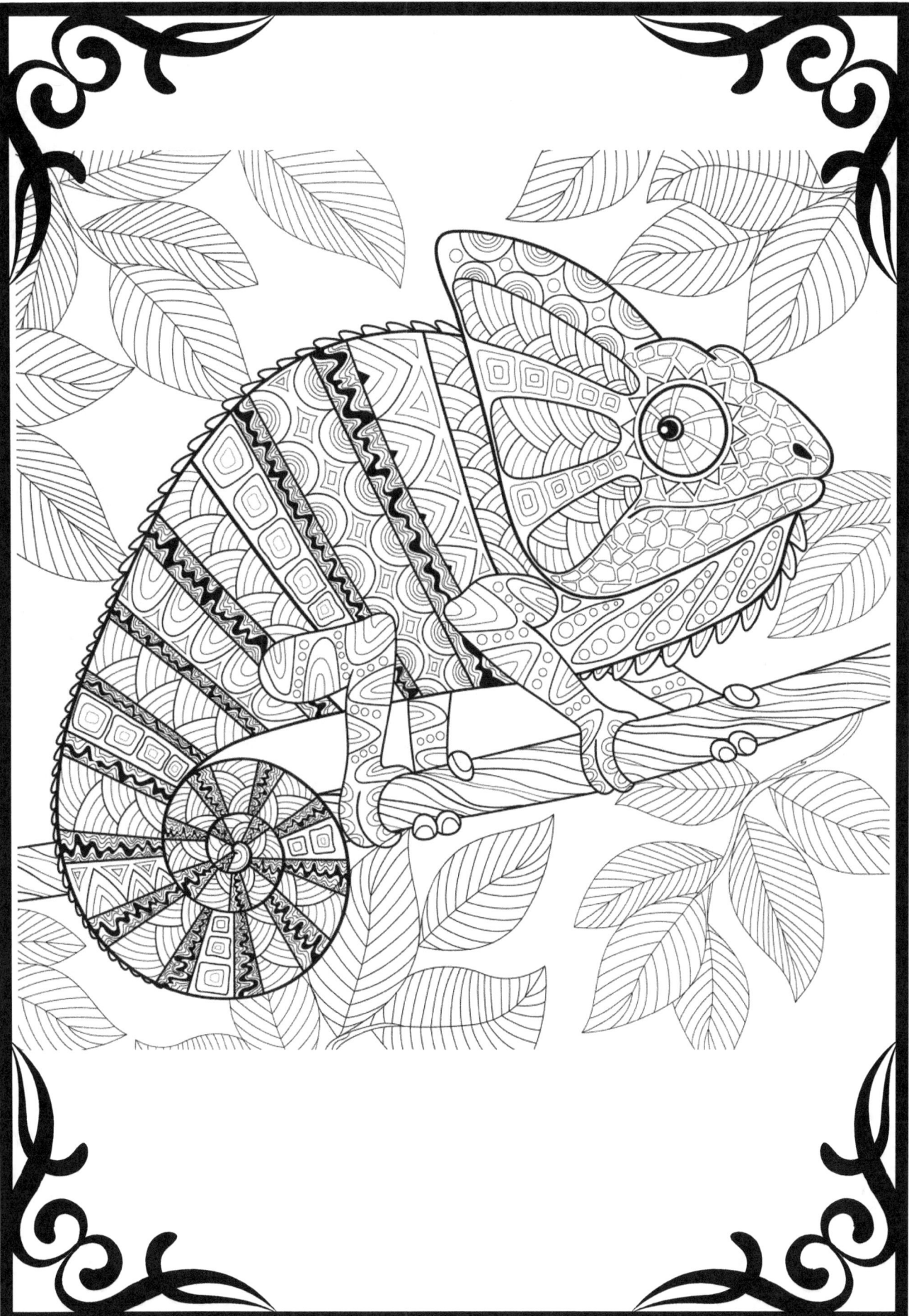

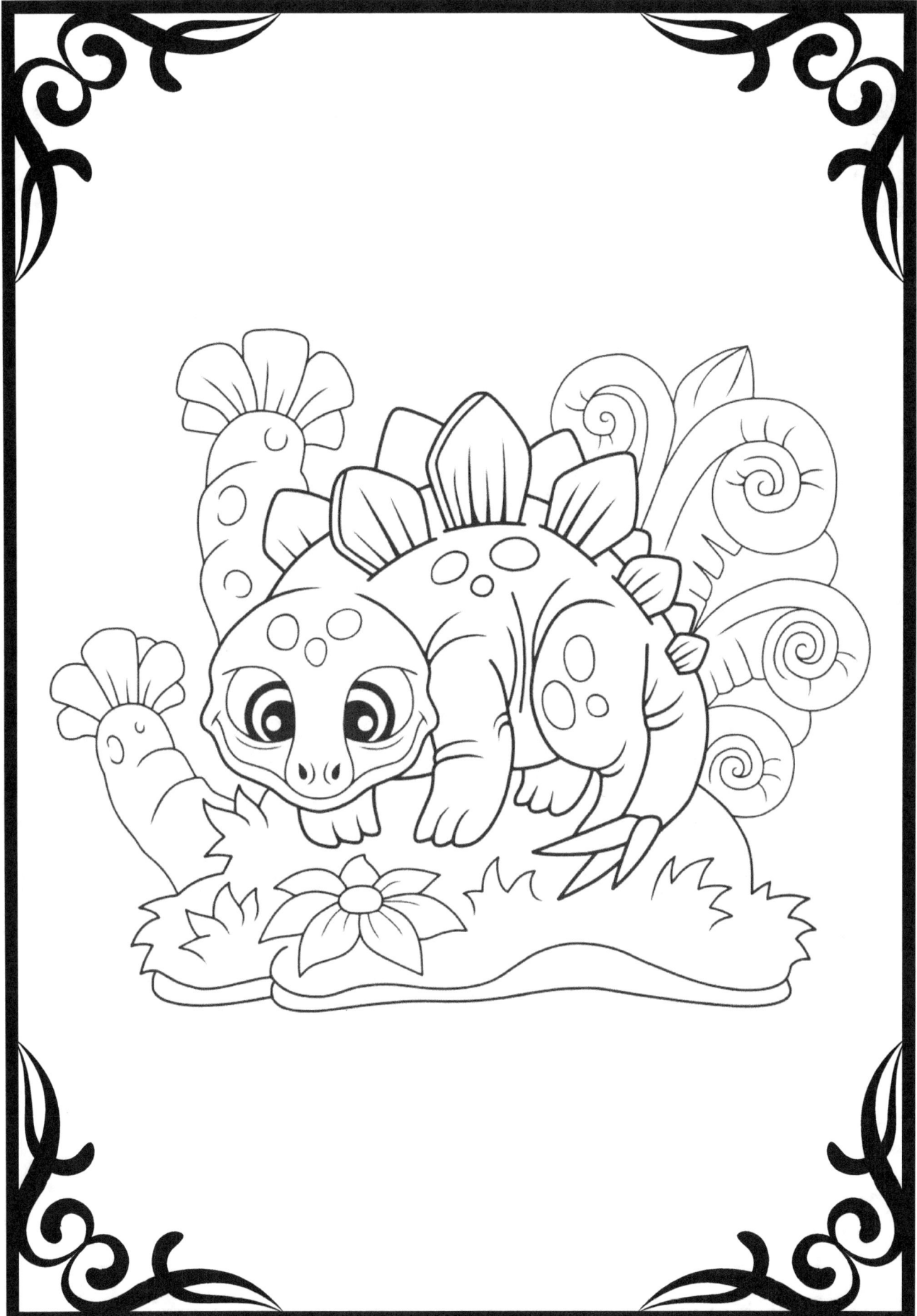

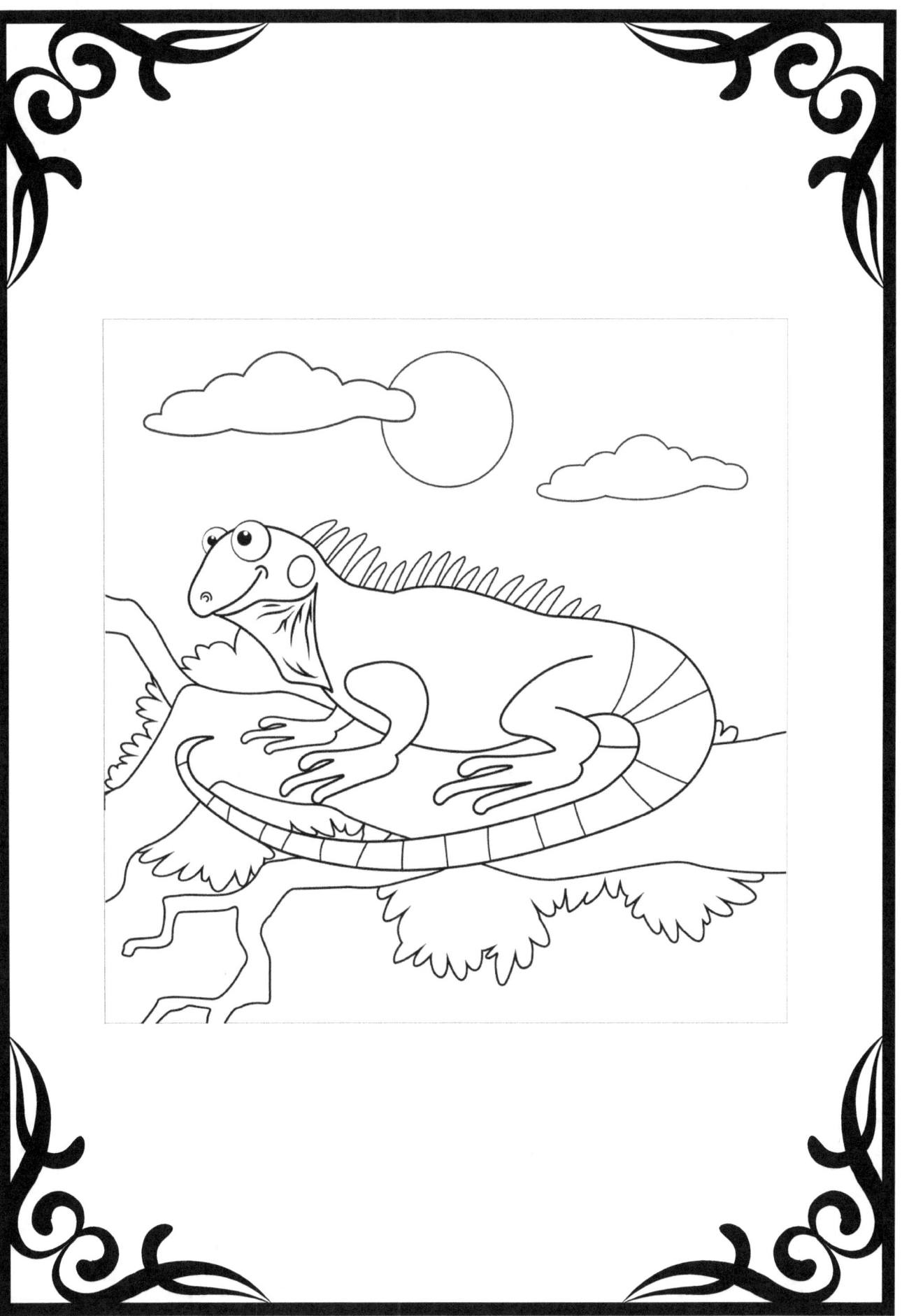

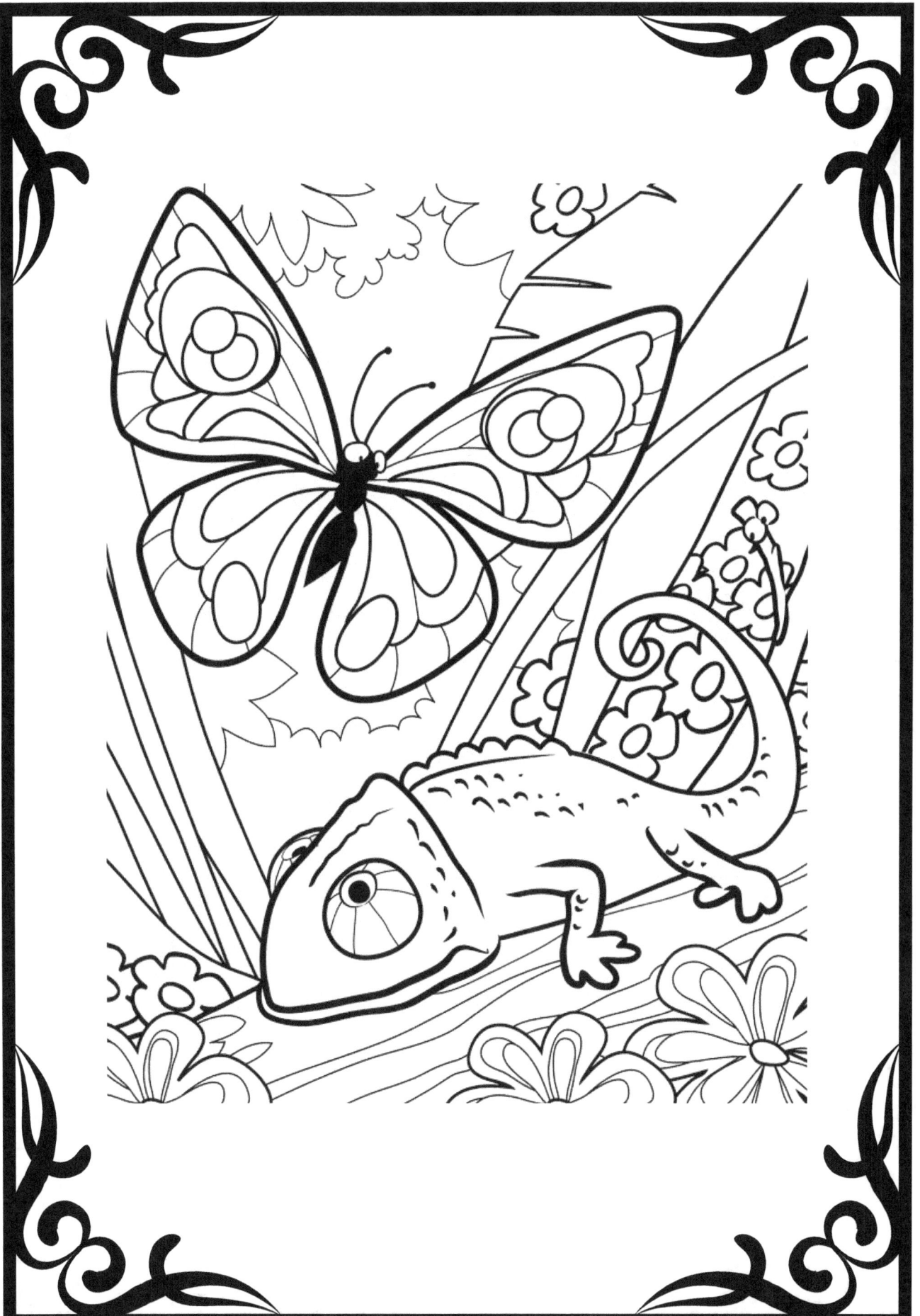

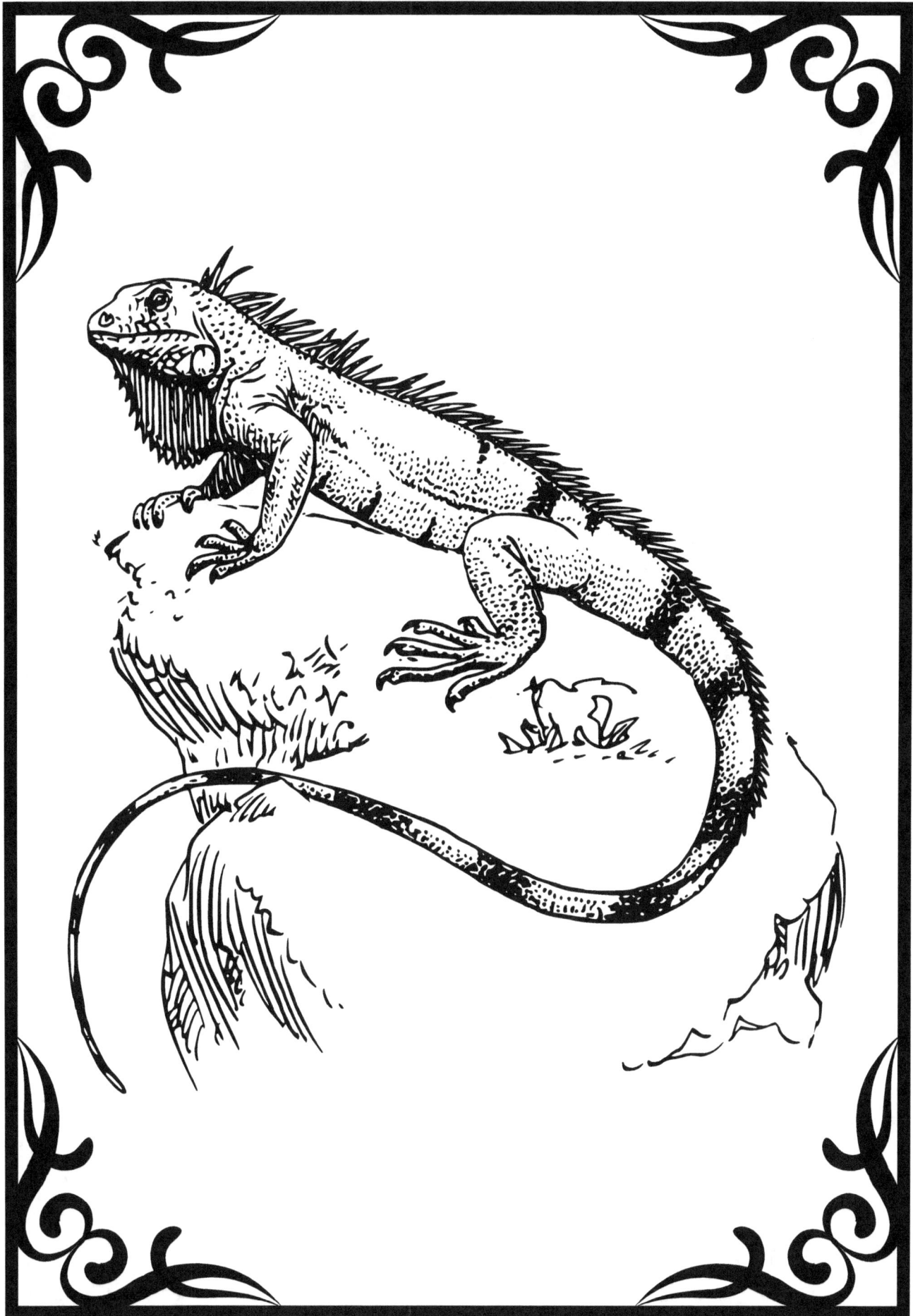

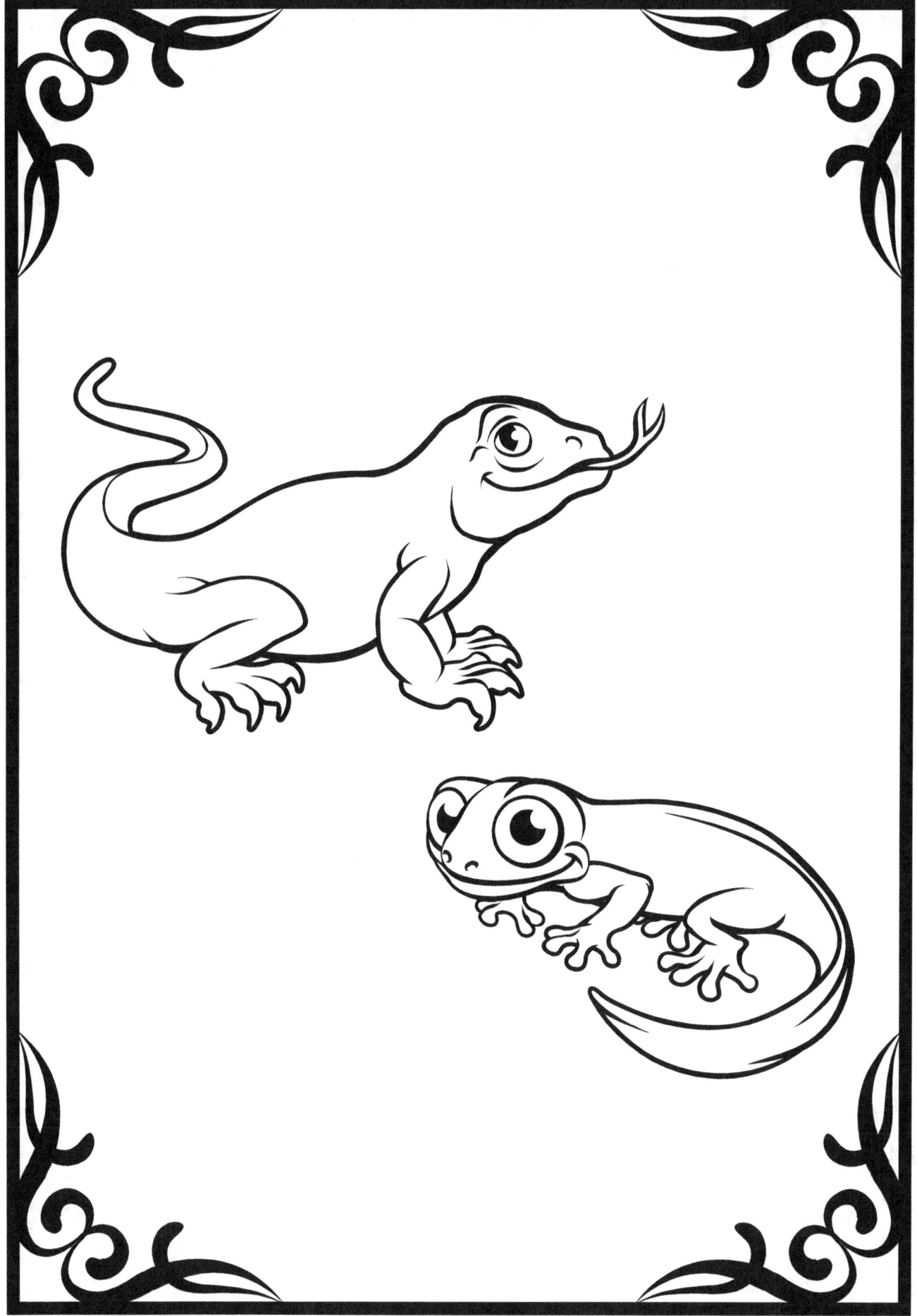

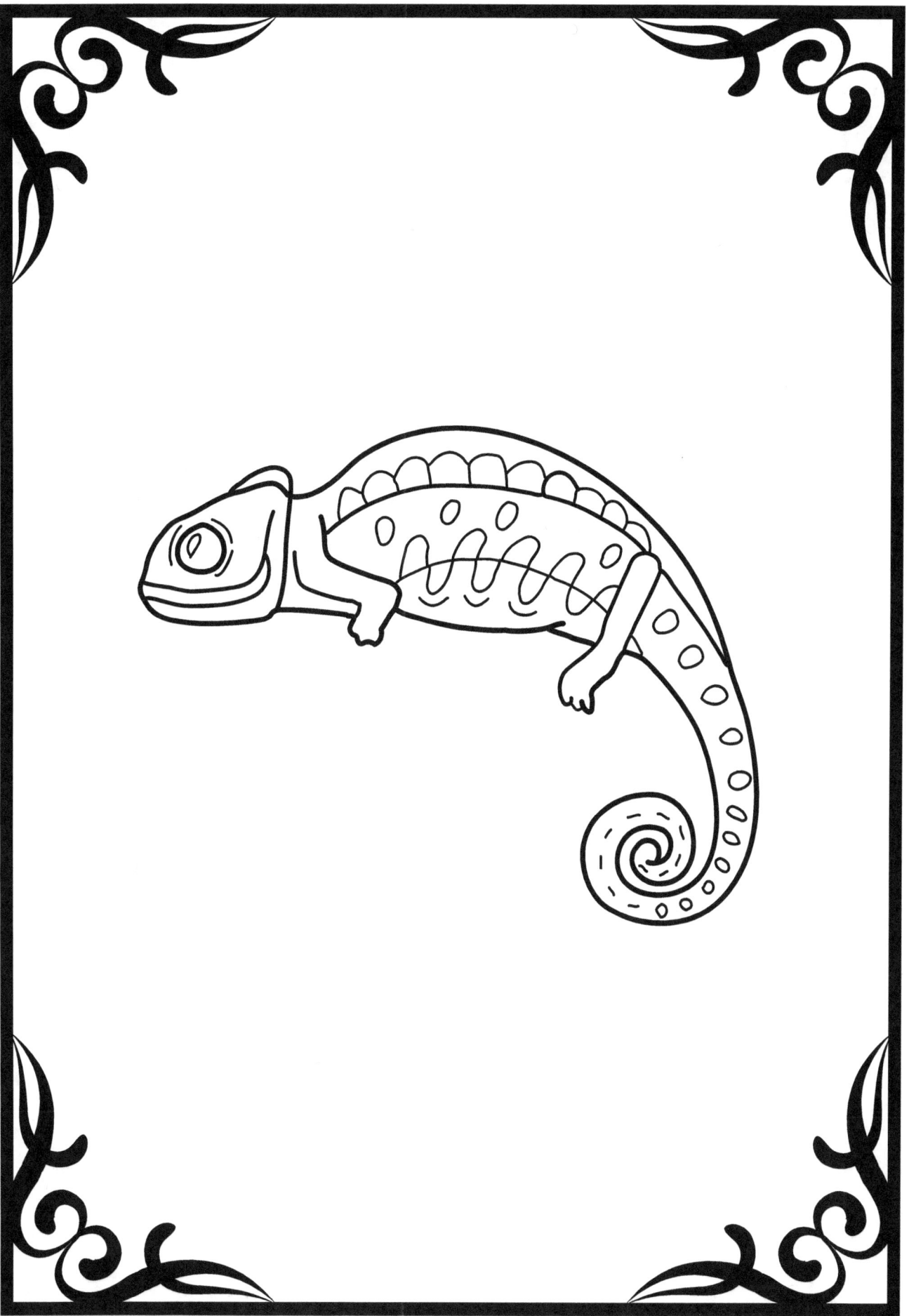

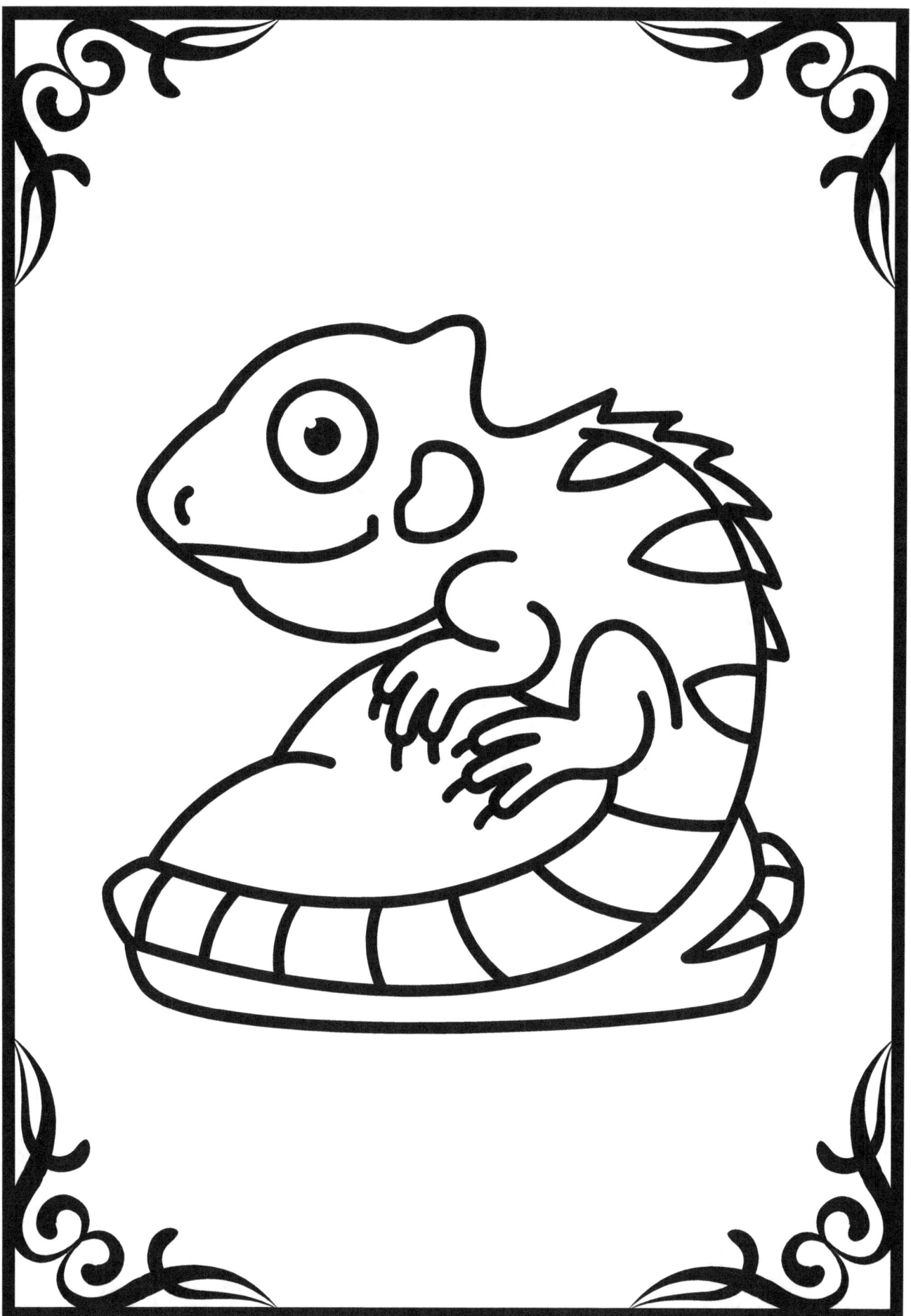

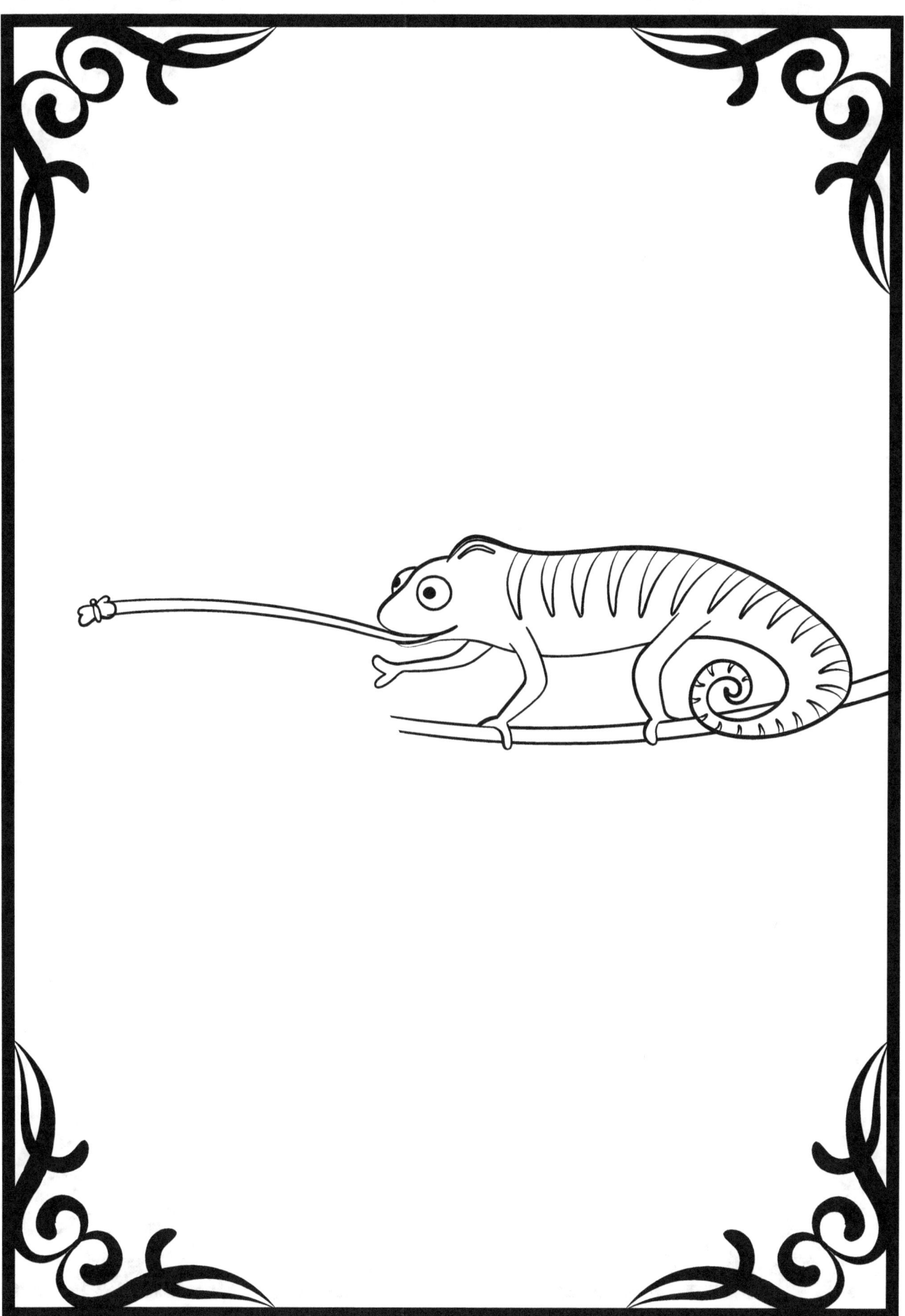

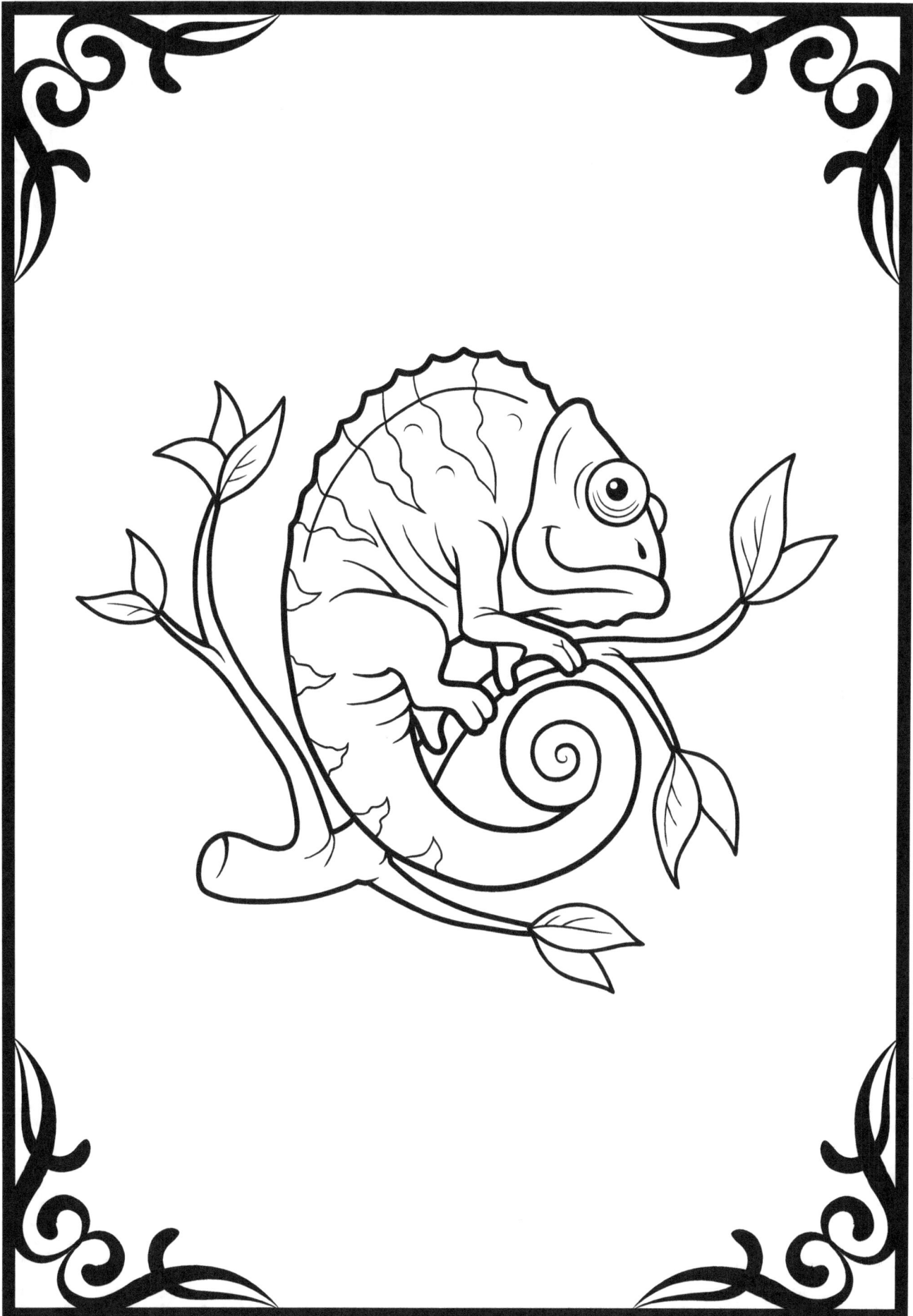

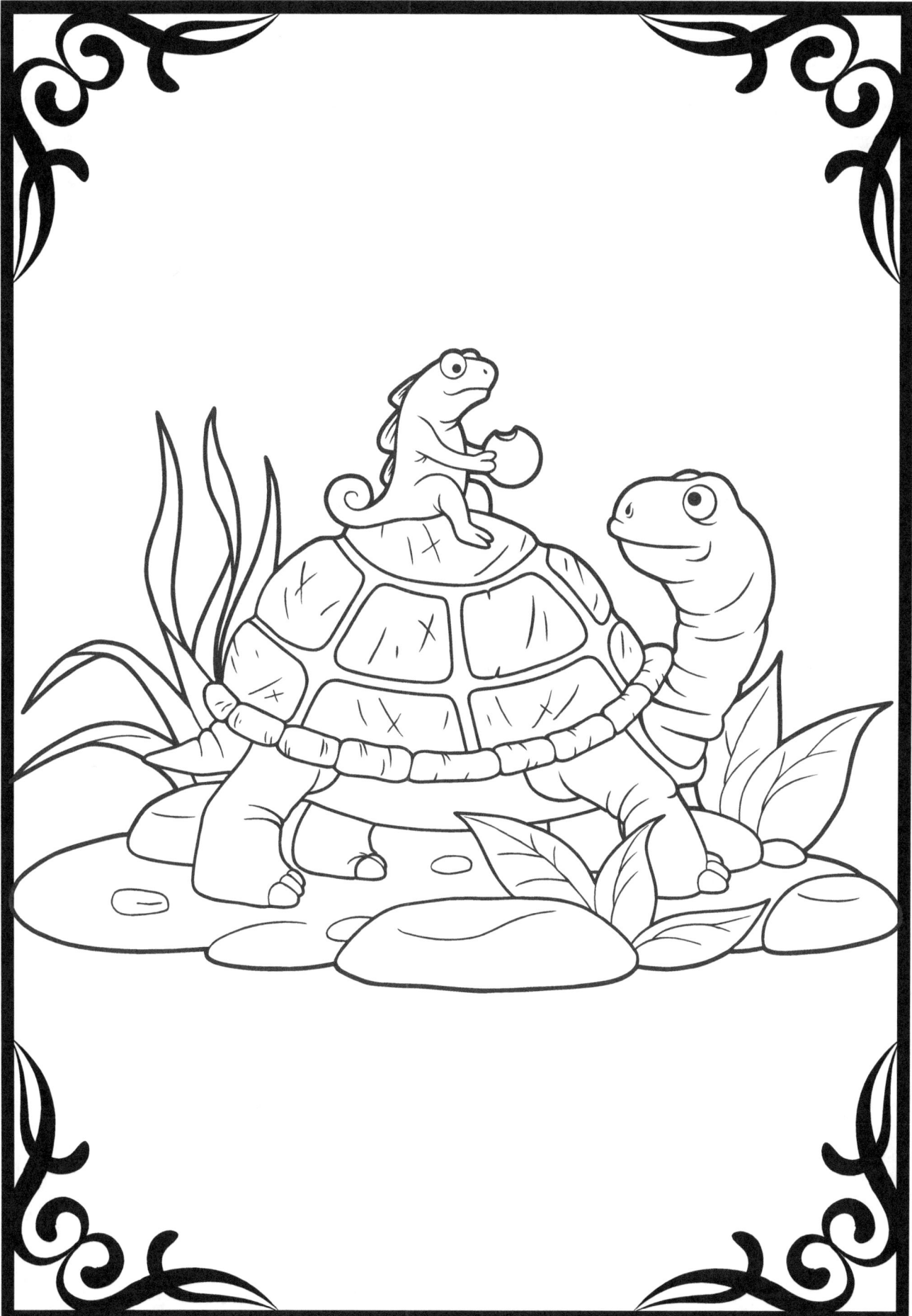

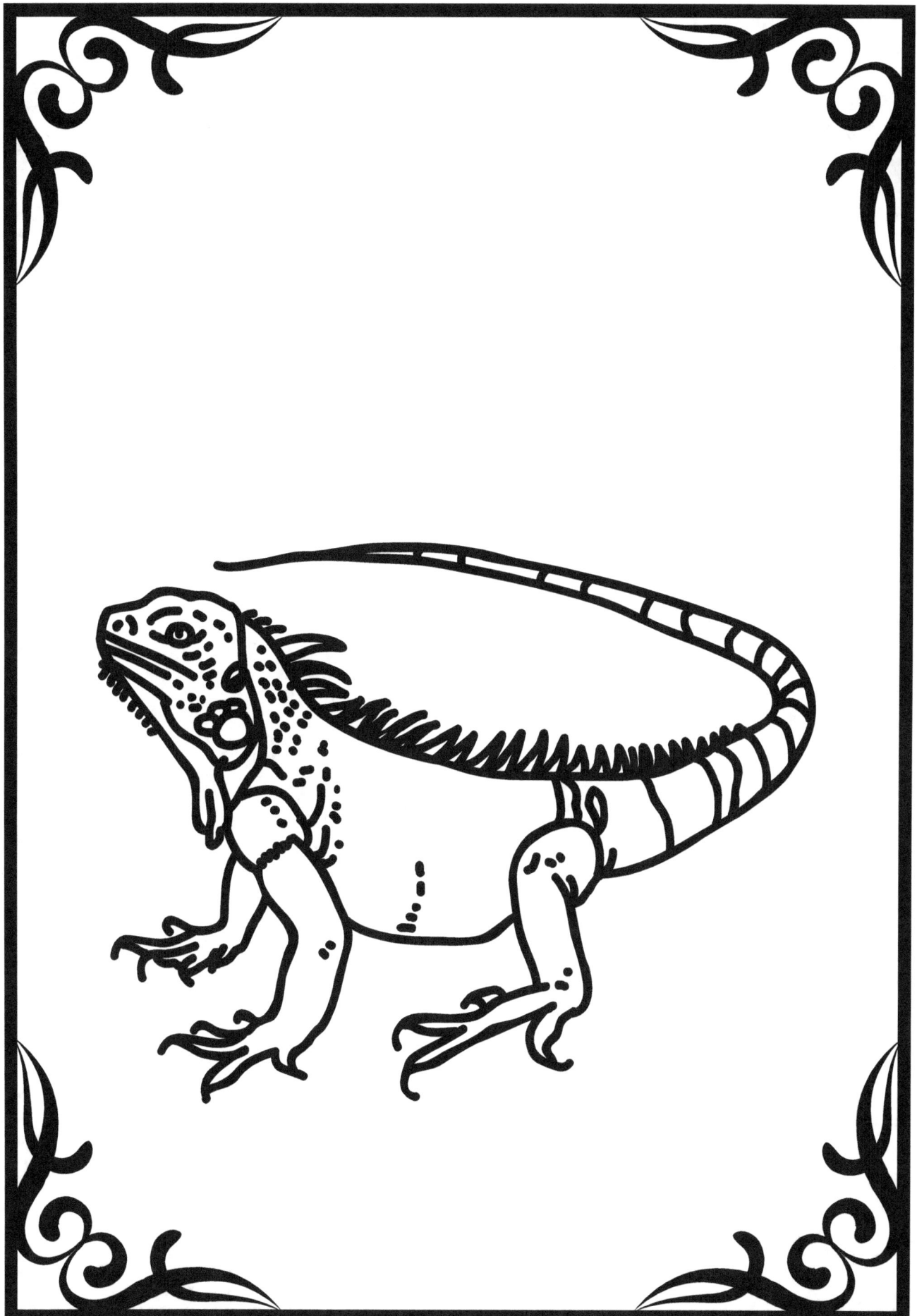

www.ingramcontent.com/pod-product-compliance
Lightning Source LLC
Chambersburg PA
CBHW082120220526
45472CB00009B/2248